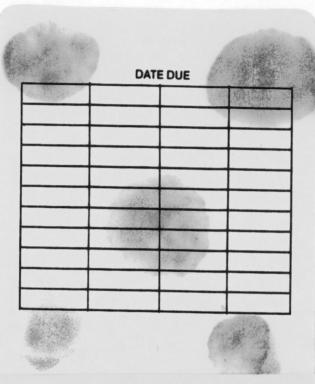

DATE DUE

808   Quilliam, S.
Q   1001 essay titles

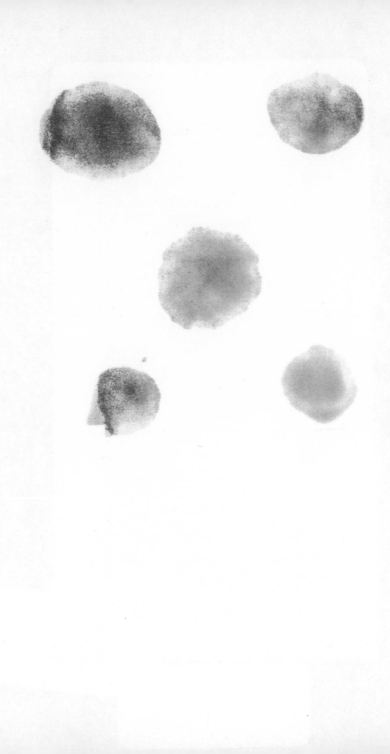

1001
Essay Titles

Susan Quilliam

James Nisbet

This book grew out of a real need – the need, in the classroom, for a seemingly endless supply of good, strong essay titles. Beginning-of-term assessments or mid-year exams include essay papers. The latest classroom project needs to be supplemented with creative assignments. The composition lesson ends – and the search for homework questions begins!

So 1001 Essay Titles was written. It contains a variety of essay questions of all types, providing opportunities for imaginative writing and simple discursive and argumentative work. You can use the book for most age and ability ranges in the middle and secondary school, though it's particularly suitable up to pre-C.S.E. and O level work.

The main part of the book, pages 4-27, gives essays listed in subject order. Each subject group begins with one-word starters and progresses to more developed questions. A variety of ways of looking at the topic – and chances to use a variety of writing styles – are included in each group.

Pages 28-32 provide shorter, more open-ended titles. These, particularly the starter sentences, are very useful for assessment work, because the freedom to develop the question as they want allows students to show their own capabilities clearly.

1001 Essay Titles is designed to be used in many ways. Use simpler titles to consolidate learning, more difficult ones to stretch ability. Mix questions from different subject areas, or set a number of questions from one section to provide different approaches to the same subject. Vary the open-ended titles by adding a definite or indefinite article or an exclamation or question mark. Mix titles – one-worders, starter sentences and more developed questions – for a soundly balanced assessment or exam.

So although 1001 titles is not an endless supply, it will help to make the search for good, strong essay questions simpler, shorter – and a lot more fun!

If your need is for letter questions, try the companion book, 333 Letter Questions, by Susan Quilliam.

Published by James Nisbet & Co. Ltd, Welwyn Garden City, Herts
First Published 1983 © Susan Quilliam 07202 0840 8

Typesetting by Word Perfect Typesetting Ltd, St Albans, Herts

8/85 KENT £ 1.40

2

CONTENTS

Animals

1. Wild Animal
2. Pounce!
3. Migration
4. Creepy Crawlies
5. Safari
6. Monster
7. Prowl
8. Prey
9. Rats!
10. My favourite pet.
11. Write a story beginning, "The note in the pet shop window read: Good home wanted for unusual pet."
12. "It slithered towards me, hissing . . ." Write about the ideas that these words bring to mind.
13. "You never forget your very first pet!" Do you? Did you?
14. Which animal do these words remind you of? Write a description of, or a story based around, the animal you choose.
    a. fierce, majestic, prowling   b. cuddly, furry, big-eyed
15. "Zoos are not to keep animals in but to keep people out." What is your view of zoos?
16. Pretend you are an animal in a zoo. Describe a day in your life.
17. "If I could talk to the animals . . ." Today, you can talk to any animal you like. Which animal would you choose? What would you say?
18. Imagine you are a racing pigeon just released. What happens to you on your way home?
19. Some people think that killing animals for their meat and fur is wrong. What do you think?
20. You are *either* a South Atlantic whale fisherman *or* a member of the Save the Whales society. Explain your point of view.
21. You wake up tomorrow morning and find that you've changed overnight into *either* a spider *or* a boa constrictor. Describe your first day.
22. If you could have any animal you wanted as a pet, which would you choose? *Either* explain why you have chosen this one *or* write about the problems you might have looking after it.
23. Your next-door neighbour is illtreating his Alsatian puppy. You and your friends decide to do something about it. Carry on the story.
24. It's the year 3000 and you're going to spend the day at the zoo – on Mars! Describe your day.
25. You step into a time warp and find yourself in the primeval forests facing a dinosaur. What happens next?

26. Fame!
27. Dress Rehearsal
28. Audition
29. Opening Night
30. Harmony
31. The Band
32. Curtain Call
33. The Fan
34. Encore!
35. My kind of music
36. That's Entertainment!
37. My favourite record
38. The School Choir
39. A Star is Born
40. This is Your Life!
41. Write a story including these words, "The sound of music filled my ears."
42. You've just attended your first audition and been immediately snapped up by the manager of the country's top group to replace the player who's left. Carry on the story from there.
43. Describe a concert or gig that you have recently attended.
44. "I've only ever wanted to do one thing in my life, and that's dance!" What do these words bring to mind?
45. Have you ever been involved in producing or acting in a play? Describe how you felt before the performance, during and after it.
46. "I just know everything's going to go wrong!" Write a story from the point of view of an actor, musician or dancer who is convinced that his or her performance will be a disaster.
47. The worst actor in the world (school, college, neighbourhood).
48. Imagine that you could choose three records to take with you to a desert island. Which would you take and why?
49. Write a story in which one of the following plays an important part: a guitar, a stage dagger, an understudy.
50 Discuss your tastes in either music or art.
51. Do you have a favourite picture? Describe it and say why you like it.
52. Some people say that too much money is spent on subsidising the arts. What do you think?
53. A ballet dancer and a boxer are trapped in a lift together. Describe the conversation they have while waiting to be rescued.
54. Why spend money on a theatre ticket when you could go to a football match?
55. You've managed to sneak backstage during the performance of a concert (play, ballet). The star takes the final applause, comes off stage, and suddenly looks straight at you. What happens next?

Celebration/Childhood

56. Celebration   57. Jubilee   58. Birthdays
59. Good news   60. School Dance   61. Coming of Age
62. Coronation   63. Party Time   64. Centenary
65. An Unusual Celebration   66. The Worst Christmas Ever
67. Grandma's Ruby Wedding   68. Harvest Festival
69. Describe a christening that went wrong.
70. A party I'll never forget.
71. There was I, waiting at the church . . .
72. Write a story beginning, "I've never been so happy in my life."
73. Write a story or description including two of the following: a cake, a sing-song, dancing, a toast.
74. Describe a scene where almost everybody is celebrating.
75. "We won!" How did you celebrate?
76. "As soon as I saw the envelope, I knew it contained the results. I slowly drew the paper out – I'd passed!" Continue the story.
77. Write about a time when you celebrated on your own.
78. For the Queen's hundredth birthday, everyone has the day off. How do you spend your day?
79. "I've got the job!" Carry on from there.
80. Write a story beginning, " 'Have you heard the news?' she asked."
81. The Lost Child   82. My First Memory   83. Baby-Sitting
84. Playground Games   85. When I was young . . .   86. Triplets!
87. "I love you but I don't like you . . ." What is your view of your relations?
88. Childhood is the happiest time of your life. Do you agree?
89. "The small boy looked up at me trustingly and smiled." Carry on with this story.
90. Jonathan is six. He has fair hair, blue eyes and an angelic face. He is also the worst ruffian in the school. Write a story about him.
91. Is adoption a good idea or not?
92. All the children in the world have joined a society and you are the president. What would you like the society to achieve? What could it contribute to the world?
93. Pretend you are a parent. Describe your children on a good day, and then on a bad day!

94. Day Trip   95. Wilderness   96. The Cliff
97. Trees   98. Sand Dunes   99. Landslide
100. View from the Top   101. Parks are for Posing!
102. Don't Walk on the Grass!   103. A Journey Through the Woods
104. Describe a country scene you remember.
105. Write a story which includes the following: a cottage, a new-born calf, mud, a flood.
106. "The land was totally changed. You wouldn't have believed you were in England."
107. It is a hot sunny day. You are out walking in the country. Suddenly you hear a strange noise. What happens next?
108. You've been asked to write a report for the local tourist guide on one aspect of the countryside you particularly enjoy. What do you write?
109. Write a story ending with these words, "I stared around at the landscape. How could I ever have thought it boring?"
110. Whilst in the park, you absent-mindedly chew a piece of strange-looking leaf and are reduced to 15 cm in height. Describe your experiences.
111. This morning when you woke, you discovered you'd slipped through time and were lying on the site of your house twenty thousand years ago. What did you see? What happened to you then?
112. Choose a scene that might include these things: sand, rocks, heat, sun. Describe it, trying to make the reader see your scene.
113. Do you think we need more countryside or less?
114. "We always used to call it 'Our Park', even though it was only a bit of grass and a few trees between the houses. To us, it was special."
115. "Trees always frighten me. They're like people listening to what you say."
116. "Carpets of fallen leaves, red, brown and yellow . . ." What do these words bring to mind?
117. "The Creepers are coming!" Write a horror story based on these words.
118. One day, you think you see a tree get up and walk a few metres before settling to the ground again. Carry on the story from there.

Crisis

119. Emergency   120. The Quarrel   121. Break-up
122. Changes   123. Disaster   124. Crash!
125. Invasion   126. Take me to your Leader!
127. What has been the biggest crisis in your life so far?
128. "I never want to see you again!" she screamed.
129. You are driving, or being driven, along the fast lane of a motorway, when suddenly the car in front of you swerves into your path. What happens next?
130. Your best friend has just split up with his or her girl or boy friend and is telling you all about it. Describe the conversation.
131. "She looked out of the window, over to the sandpit where the children were playing. 'Oh, no!' she said . . ." Continue this story.
132. You return home one evening to find that a member of your family has been rushed to hospital. What happens next? How do you react? How do you feel?
133. "Sit down," said Dad, slowly. "I've got some bad news for you."
134. Describe what happened when a friend told you a few home truths.
135. The local factory has just announced that it is closing down. Describe what the effects are on your family and how you cope.
136. At eleven o'clock one night, your elder brother or sister comes in. Ten minutes later, there's a knock on the door and it's the police. What happens next?
137. Write a story about a crisis which affects everyone in your street.
138. You wake up one morning to find that the whole world has changed overnight. How and why? What happens?
139. The day that war broke out.
140. "I always remember," said Grandad, "the most important thing that ever happened to me . . ." Tell the story that Grandad told.
141. "We just won't stand for it," said Maggie. "They can't do this to us."
142. Write about a time you learned a lesson.
143. "I'm afraid," he said sternly, "I'm going to have to ask you to leave." What do these words bring to mind?
144. Choose one of the following and write about what effect it would have on the world: a plague of ants, a Martian landing, a virus which rots metal. Write either an article or a story.

145. Homework   146. Examinations   147. Detention
148. Playing Truant   149. School's for Fools   150. My Ideal School
151. Parent-Teacher Evening   152. First Day at School
153. Corporal Punishment – Yes or No?
154. School ends, learning begins.
155. Your local Students' Union is meeting to discuss changes and improvements. Suggest three improvements that could be made to our education system.
156. Which was your happiest year at school? Why?
157. For one day, you are the teacher and the teachers in your school are the pupils. Describe what happens.
158. What is the most important thing you've learned since starting school?
159. It's the year 2500. Describe a typical school day.
160. You're visiting a penfriend in a foreign country. He or she suggests you go to the local school for the day. Describe your experiences.
161. Which subjects would you prefer to learn rather than the normal school subjects? Why?
162. "I'd rather die than sit another exam!" How do you see exams?
163. Write a story including one of these: a school bully, a teacher who can't keep control, a dinner lady with a problem.
164. "The doors, huge and menacing, gaped wide. The sign over the door read 'Moss Street School'. Summoning up all my courage, I went in." What happens next?
165. "So," said the Headmaster, "you've been caught in the act. Well, I warned you." Write two endings to this story, one happy, one sad.
166. The advantages and disadvantages of a very large (or small) school.
167. Many schools abroad start their day at 8.30 a.m. and finish at 1.30 p.m. with no lunch break. Argue *either* for *or* against introducing a similar system to your school.
168. Your head teacher has asked for views on whether pupils should wear school uniform or not. Write about your opinion.
169. "Community schools integrate the classroom and the community." "I'd hate to have my Mum studying English in the same room as me." What do you think?
170. Write a story about a school that is being forced to close.

Family

171. The New Baby   172. Family Holidays   173. Relatives!
174. I wish I was an only child.   175. Family of the Future
176. I hate big brothers!   177. Family Shopping
178. Big families are best.   179. The happiest family I know
180. My least favourite relative
181. "I'd like my Mum and Dad if they weren't my parents." What thoughts does this statement bring to mind?
182. Describe a member of your family whom you find interesting, explaining what makes him or her so.
183. A relative you've never met before is visiting from abroad. Describe what happens.
184. Write about what happened when you found you had a long lost brother or sister.
185. Write a story beginning with the words, "That's it," said Mum. "I'm fed up with this family!"
186. Write a story which includes one of the following: a family quarrel, an adopted child, a family tree.
187. You stay with a friend's family for the weekend. What happens?
188. "I love my children dearly, but sometimes I wish I could send them back."
189. "We knew there would be trouble when Granny came to stay."
190. "I'd like to change my family." What would your ideal family be like?
191. The average family in the Western world has two or three children. Do you think this is too large a family or too small? Give reasons for your view.
192. "Ah!" cried the Count, "I always knew I'd find my long-lost child one day!" Write a story that includes these words.
193. Communes are places where several families live together. What do you think would be the advantages and disadvantages of living in a commune?
194. "Our family gets together at Christmas. The result is marvellous chaos!" Write about the times when all your family get together.
195. Write about a happy memory you have of your family.
196. You come home one evening to find your house in darkness. As you open the sitting-room door, to your surprise, you find all the family there sitting waiting for you. What happens next?

197. Apology
198. Waiting
199. Afraid!
200. Prejudice
201. Temper Tantrum
202. Homesickness
203. Panic
204. Despair
205. Boasting
206. Disappointment
207. Regret
208. Pretend . . .
209. Right now, I feel . . .
210. I feel silly when . . .
211. What are your feelings about a change you have experienced in your life?
212. Write about a time when you were upset.
213. Write a story in which someone is very happy.
214. Write a story about a future or alien world in which people have no emotions.
215. "I've never been so embarrassed in my life!"
216. "She just laughed and laughed."
217. Describe your feelings when you see or hear about one of the following: a new baby, a motorbike or car accident, an exam failure.
218. Write a story ending with the sentence, "I knew I'd never feel the same again."
219. Curiosity killed the cat. Write about someone who is curious.
220. "All of a sudden, Jo burst into tears." What happened next?
221. Pretend you have more power than anyone else in the world. How would you feel? What would you do?
222. Write about a time you hoped for something and were disappointed, or did not expect something and were pleasantly surprised.
223. I never thought I'd hate anyone in my life, but . . .
224. Write about an occasion when you were envious or jealous.
225. Choose one of the following and write about your feelings, good and bad, towards that person: your best friend, your head teacher, your dentist.
226. Write a story including the words, " 'You'd feel better if you threw something,' he said."
227. You wake up to find you can't understand what anyone is saying, and they can't understand you. Describe your feelings.
228. "I felt myself slipping away . . ."
229. "Slowly, the door opened . . ."
230. Write about what you think and feel when attending a party.

Food and Drink

231. School Dinners   232. The Picnic   233. The Banquet
234. Barbecue   235. Famine   236. Toothache
237. Food for Thought   238. T.V. Dinners   239. My favourite meal
240. You can choose anywhere in the world you want to have a meal. Where do you go and what do you eat?
241. Cabbage, spinach, semolina pudding: write about some foods you hate.
242. "Dad (or Mum) is on a diet again!" Has anyone in your family been on a diet? What happened?
243. " 'I suppose it'll taste all right,' she said doubtfully." Write a story including these words.
244. Write a story including one or more of these: a take-away meal, tomato ketchup, a bottle of lemonade, a knickerbocker glory.
245. "Just at that moment, she nudged my elbow, and a whole packet of curry powder tipped into the pan . . ." Continue the story.
246. Write about a meal that was a total disaster.
247. Write about a person who eats too much.
248. The Pie Eating Competition.
249. What do you think we'll be eating and drinking in five hundred years' time? Describe a typical meal.
250. "I never thought I'd be eating jam sandwiches in the best restaurant in town!" Write a story including these words.
251. You go for a meal and then realise you haven't enough money to pay the bill. What happens next?
252. Write a story beginning with the words, "As I watched, he opened the boot of his car to reveal what looked like a tonne of spaghetti!"
253. Imagine you're either a cook in a famous restaurant or a cook in a school canteen. Describe your day.
254. Some people think that soon there won't be enough food left to feed cattle and we will all have to become vegetarians. What is your reaction to this thought?
255. Write a story about a mad cook, a coach load of ravenous tourists and no food.
256. Write about a time when you were really hungry or thirsty.
257. "Slowly, the tray tilted and fourteen glasses of champagne crashed to the floor!" Write a story including these words.

258. Disco
259. Window-Shopping
260. The Youth Club
261. Evening Class
262. Posers
263. The Playground
264. Visiting Relatives
265. Walking the Dog
266. A Day Out
267. How do you spend your weekend?
268. Tell the story of a Saturday night out that went wrong.
269. Write about something you wish you'd invented.
270. Write a story including one of the following: a race, a show, a team, an audience.
271. Have you ever spent a day completely on your own? Write about your experiences and feelings.
272. The rewards and problems of *either* cycling *or* photography *or* growing plants *or* keeping pets.
273. You've just read a book/seen a film/bought a good album. Recommend it to a friend, explaining why you liked it.
274. How do you think people will spend their free time a hundred years from now?
275. "I'm bored! I'm bored!" Write about whatever those words make you think or feel.
276. Have you ever collected money for charity? Write about some of the experiences of *either* a door-to-door collector *or* a flag seller.
277. "What on earth are we going to do?" Carry on the story from there.
278. Write about a party you gave or attended which was *either* a roaring success *or* a total failure.
279. "Young people waste their free time; they should be encouraged to do something useful." How would you react to these words?
280. Pretend you are an overworked parent. Describe your experiences trying to keep a large family amused during the summer holidays.
281. Write a story ending with these words. "That's the last time I let you decide what we do on Sundays!"
282. Write about someone you know who has an unusual hobby. Why does he or she like it?
283. Write about a typical Saturday morning in your family.
284. "Why do the summer holidays seem two years long at the beginning and two days long by the end?" Describe some of your experiences of summer holidays.

Houses and Homes

285. The Deserted House
286. Leaving Home
287. My Ideal House
288. The Housing Estate
289. Moving Day
290. Redecorating
291. Underground House
292. Living in Space
293. Home, Sweet Home
294. I live in a Castle.
295. A Room With a View
296. You travel back in time and find yourself living in one of these homes: a Stone Age cave, an igloo, a Red Indian tent, a wattle and daub cottage, an Elizabethan manor house, a Mongol yurt. Write about your experiences.
297. You wake up to find yourself living in the year 2200. Describe your house, outside and inside.
298. Write a story beginning, "It was the strangest house I'd ever seen."
299. Write a story ending, "As he reached the gate, he turned back for a last, long look at the house."
300. Write a story including two or more of the following: an attic, a dark cellar, a steep staircase, an open window, a secret door, a chandelier, a four-poster bed.
301. "I don't just want a house, I want a home!"
302. You turn the corner and walk down your road. Where your house used to be, there is a totally new building you've never seen. What happens next?
303. "Look out!" yelled Tracey. "There goes the paint pot!" Carry on with this story.
304. "That's the seventeenth house we've seen today, and my feet hurt!" Have you ever been house hunting? What happened?
305. Dust, damp, creaks overhead. Write about any thoughts or memories these words bring to mind.
306. "High-rise blocks are the destroyers of modern life." What is your view of tower blocks?
307. "When I was young, our house was as big as a palace. Now I'm older, it's shrunk to the size of a shed!" Write about your first memories of a house where you lived. Has your view changed over the years?
308. The Council is planning to demolish your street. What arguments could you put forward to persuade it to change its decision?
309. You arrive home from school to find that a tribe of chimpanzees has taken over your house. What happens next?

310. Dream Machine   311. Gadgets   312. The Mechanic
313. Blackout   314. Production Line   315. Trouble-Shooter
316. Blow-Up   317. Breakdown   318. The Live Wire
319. Ghost in the Machine   320. It won't work!
321. Do you think machines could ever replace human beings?
322. Write about a world where robots are in charge.
323. Write a story about a robot that went wrong.
324. You have designed a marvellous new invention called a grunge sprocket. What is it, what does it do, how does it work?
325. Due to a slight slip in a time warp, you find yourself living in a world where the wheel has not yet been invented. Describe your experiences.
326. A Martian has landed on earth and wants to know what the things around him do. Explain to him at least one of the following: a washing machine, a hairdryer, a Space Invaders machine, a digital alarm watch.
327. Write a story including one of the following: a forklift truck, a bicycle, a pocket calculator, a video tape recorder.
328. Choose one or more of these words and use them in a description of or story about a machine: humming, deafening, spinning, rumbling, roaring, sliding.
329. Write a story about a conversation with a computer.
330. "All of a sudden, with no warning, the machine started to move." What happens next?
331. What one machine would you most miss if it disappeared from the world? Give the reasons for your choice.
332. Imagine you wake up 7 cm. tall and trapped in either your television or your fridge. Carry on the story from there.
333. Write a story including these words – "The machines rumbled forward; on and on they came."
334. "Come on," he said, sliding into the ventilation shaft, "it's the only way out." Carry on the story from there.
335. Every time you take a picture with your camera, you get a photo of something that wasn't there. Carry on with this story.
336. Your pocket calculator starts to talk to you. What does it say?

Media

337. Headline! 338. Take Five 339. On the Air
340. Front Page 341. News Flash 342. The Reporter
343. The Hit Story 344. One More Time! 345. The Director's Chair
346. My favourite programme 347. The T.V. that talked
348. Advertisements I like 349. Local Radio – for or against?
350. Write a story in which a radio ham plays an important part.
351. Choose your favourite magazine and explain why you like it.
352. Without telling the story, explain why you like your favourite film.
353. Do you think television is taking over our lives?
354. Choose an advertisement you disapprove of and explain why you dislike it.
355. Pretend you are a famous film star. Which film would you most like to star in? Who would you choose as your supporting cast?
356. Write a story about a reporter, an editor and four thousand newspapers.
357. You have half an hour of T.V. time to express your point of view about any issue. Which issue would you choose and how would you use your time?
358. Write a story to fit this headline – The Vanishing Star.
359. Which do you prefer – going to the cinema or watching a film at home? Why?
360. Argue for or against censorship in the media.
361. "Quiz shows are an insult to anyone's intelligence." What do you think?
362. "That's the worst film I've ever seen!" Continue the story.
363. You are a radio disc jockey for the day. Describe your experiences.
364. Write a story including the words, "She ripped the newspaper to shreds."
365. Write about your first day at work as a reporter for the local paper.
366. "Very faintly, through the crackling, came a desperate voice. Then the radio died completely." What happened next?
367. Plan an ideal evening's television viewing for yourself.
368. Write a story about a community newspaper that wins a battle.
369. Write a story about someone who became a celebrity for a day.
370. What would happen if mass communication was banned in the world from today on?

371. Alibi
372. Beware!
373. The Dare
374. Fugitive
375. Hostage
376. Revolution
377. Stop!
378. The Witch
379. The Mob
380. Adventure
381. Truce!
382. Smugglers
383. Ghosts
384. The Phantom Robot
385. Missing!
386. Things that go bump in the night.
387. Whilst baby-sitting, you hear a strange noise upstairs. What happens next?
388. "Shaking, he pulled out a gun. 'You'll never stop me,' he snarled."
389. Write a story about what these words bring to mind: mist, howl, creep.
390. Pretend you have just seen a crime committed. What do you do?
391. The car swung away in a tight turn, its brakes squealing . . . What happens next?
392. Write a story including two of the following: a fingerprint, a secret message, a train journey.
393. "Well Watson," said Sherlock Holmes, "it all looks very clear to me." Write a story including these words.
394. Choose three of the following words and use them in a story: spirit, fear, grave, strange, crawling, insect.
395. "I never want to see another ghost again." Write a story ending in these words.
396. Write a mystery story, set either a hundred years in the past or a hundred years in the future.
397. Pretend you are an investigator, *either* of crimes *or* of psychic happenings. Describe one of your adventures.
398. Write a story involving a code, a crime and a policeman.
399. "I just don't understand what's happened!" Write a story including these words.
400. A mad scientist has fed his formula to a cat. Next morning, all the cats in the world are six metres high. Carry on the story from there.
401. Describe your adventures as a pirate.
402. "008 frowned. The job was going to be more difficult than he thought." Carry on the story from there.
403. You are a very friendly alien landing on Earth for the first time. Describe your adventures.

People

404. The Busker   405. The Boss   406. The Neighbours
407. Bus Queue   408. The Concert   409. Riot!
410. Tourists   411. Too Many People   412. Casualty!
413. My Point of View   414. Dentist's Waiting Room
415. Station Platform   416. Shopping Precinct
417. "When they ask me what happened, I just smile . . ." Write a story including these words.
418. The Public – by a shop assistant *or* a taxi driver.
419. Describe someone you would like to meet again or someone you hope never to meet again.
420. "Suddenly her smile faded and she looked a totally different person."
421. You are travelling on a train or a bus. Describe some of the other passengers, then imagine what their characters might be.
422. Write a description of yourself *either* as it might be given in a report *or* as you think your friends might see you.
423. Write a story including any one of these people; a vicar on a skateboard, a small boy with a wedding cake, an old lady with a chain saw.
424. Choose three of these adjectives and use them in a story about a person, real or imaginary: clever, sarcastic, kind-hearted, bad-tempered, proud, serene, remote, temperamental, suspicious.
425. Write a story including these words: " – and just as I was about to apologise, she began to laugh."
426. Suppose you could be anyone you wanted. Who would you be and why?
427. You've been transported *either* backwards *or* forwards in time. Where would you go and what would you be?
428. Write a story about somebody who learnt a lesson.
429. Lots of fairytale characters could be real people today. Write the story of a present-day Cinderella, Red Riding Hood or Jack and the Beanstalk. Bring the setting and what happens up to date but make sure the moral of the story remains the same.
430. You are sitting next to someone on a train when you suddenly realise that he or she is famous. What happens next?
431. Three people are stranded on a desert island. Write about their experiences.

432. Harbour Lights   433. The Ocean   434. The Stowaway
435. Man Overboard   436. Sea Creatures   437. Currents
438. Land Ahoy!   439. The Voyage   440. Seashore
441. Iceberg!   442. I live on a boat.
443. Learning to Swim   444. A Day at the Seaside
445. Dive! Dive! Dive!   446. The Captain
447. Imagine you were the first person to row the Atlantic single-handed. Tell your story.
448. Earth becomes so overcrowded that we have to live on the sea-bed. Describe a day in your life.
449. Write a story about one of the following: a Chinese junk, a ship's cat, a sinking barge.
450. Write a story including the words, 'We're going to capsize!' he yelled.
451. Write about a cruise on an ocean liner from the point of view of a passenger *or* a member of the crew.
452. Pretend you are a diver and describe your work.
453. Choose one of these sets of words and write a description or a story including them: a. calm, drifting, plop b. crashing, surf, white.
454. "The oars drifted slowly away from us, farther and farther." What happens next?
455. You see the following advertisement: Crew wanted to take yacht from Southampton to the Bahamas. No experience needed. Describe your trip as a member of the crew.
456. Describe a ride in a speedboat.
457. "Slowly the octopus stretched out its tentacles and took a firmer grip."
458. "The realisation dawned gradually: we were trapped on the sandbanks and the tide was coming in." Continue the story.
459. Pretend you have your own yacht. Where would you sail and what would you see?
460. The biggest shark ever known to man is attacking bathers on the local beach. Write a story from this starting point.
461. You are a fisherman on a North Sea fishing fleet. Describe your most exciting trip.

Senses

462. I can see . . .   463. I Spy   464. Noise
465. Through the Looking Glass   466. Seeing is Believing
467. Talking Heads   468. Smells Fishy
469. Write a story including any object you can see from where you are now sitting.
470. Imagine you can see through walls. Write about some of your experiences.
471. "She gazed into the distance, and a terrified look passed across her face." Write a story including these words.
472. Write a story ending with the words, "All I know is," he said, "that I'll never look in a mirror again!"
473. Imagine what it must be like to be blind, and write about a day in the life of a blind person.
474. Write a story including the words, "In the distance someone was whistling . . ."
475. You wake up tomorrow to find that you are deaf. Write about your reactions.
476. Write a story including at least two of these: a high-pitched sound, a dull thud, a boom, a shot, a crackle, a crunch, a rustle.
477. You are returning home late one night when all of a sudden, behind you, you hear a low, humming sound. What happens next?
478. Write an account of a concert you have attended, describing what you heard rather than what you saw.
479. Describe the experience of waking up in the morning up to the point where you open your eyes.
480. "Soft velvet, feathers, smooth wood . . ." Write about things that are good to touch.
481. "As soon as I smelt the wood fire, I remembered being six years old, camping with my father." Are there any smells that bring back memories for you?
482. Pretend you have only your sense of smell to guide you home today. Describe your journey.
483. "I stretched out my hand into the darkness and suddenly, I felt . . ." Carry on with this story.
484. By the year 3000, we will all have developed a sixth sense. Decide what this sixth sense might be and then write a story involving it.

485. Supermarket   486. Sale!   487. Bargain
488. The Changing Room   489. School Bazaar   490. Boutique
491. The Customer   492. Pedlar   493. Department Store
494. Write about something which you have always regretted buying.
495. What do you think the shops of the future will be like? Describe a typical shopping trip in the year 2100.
496. "I only discovered the shop because I lost my way." Write a story or description beginning with these words.
497. Write a story or description containing one or more of the following: a shopping trolley, four hundred tins of baked beans, a long queue, a special offer.
498. Pretend you are one of the following and write about your experiences: a salesgirl on a cosmetics counter, a checkout assistant, a bank clerk.
499. Imagine you are on a money-no-object shopping spree. Where would you shop and what would you buy?
500. "The security manager came rushing up to me. 'Stop thief!' he shouted." What happened next?
501. "I'll always remember our little corner shop. It had a special smell, and a bell on the door that rang as you went in or out." What do these words remind you of?
502. Write about a shopping trip that went horribly wrong.
503. In some cultures, bargaining is usual. Write about a sale that was made by bargaining.
504. "No, not the tin from the bottom of the pile!"
505. Write a story or description from the point of view of *either* a shopper at a jumble sale *or* someone behind the counter.
506. Write a conversation between a shopkeeper and an awkward customer.
507. "Madam, it's just you!" Write a story including these words.
508. Have you ever bought something that you have saved for? Describe what happened, particularly how you felt.
509. Describe a shopping trip where you couldn't find anything you wanted.
510. You have won a competition. The prize is a five-minute dash around a supermarket. Describe what happens.

Sky

511. Moon Landing
512. Take-Off
513. Flying Kites
514. Clouds
515. Airport
516. Landing
517. Sunrise
518. Whirlwind
519. Balloons
520. Up, up and away
521. Bird's Eye View
522. In the middle of your plane flight you suddenly realise that all the crew members, including the pilots, have disappeared. Describe what happens next.
523. Write a story about a hang-glider.
524. It is the year 3000 and you're just off for your monthly weekend away in Lunar City. Describe your flight.
525. Write a story or description including one or more of the following: a jet plane, an electric storm, a forced landing.
526. You are taking your first parachute jump. Describe your experiences and feelings.
527. Write a description or story including at least three of these words: floating, swooping, soaring, hovering, diving, wheeling.
528. Write an account of a delayed aeroplane flight from the point of view of either a passenger or a member of the airport staff.
529. Describe an occasion when you watched the sky for a long time.
530. Write about the thoughts that come into your mind when you think of either the sun or the moon.
531. If you could fly, where would you go and what would you see?
532. Imagine you are flying over your house. Describe the view.
533. Write a story beginning with these words, "Flying, flying, all you ever think of is flying!"
534. "It slowly descended from the sky as we all watched, speechless."
535. Write a story including the words, "'Look – look up there!' he said."
536. Write about the sky you can see as you look out of your window now.
537. Tell the story of an aeroplane journey from the point of view of someone who is terrified of flying.
538. Describe a visit to another galaxy.
539. Describe a firework display, from the point of view of either a spectator or a firework.
540. Tell the story of what happened during an eclipse.

541. Teamwork
544. The Competition
547. The Trainer
550. The Games
553. Marathon
556. Sport in the 21st Century
558. My Favourite Sport
560. Sports Day

542. The Winner
545. Sailing
548. The Spectator
551. Gambling
554. Kick-Off

543. Gone Fishing
546. Racing
549. Half Time
552. Thin Ice
555. Goal!

557. Football Crazy, Football Mad
559. Run for your Life!
561. Grandstand View

562. Describe the sports facilities in your neighbourhood and say how you think they could be improved.
563. Write a story about how the game of football was invented.
564. Describe *either* a time when you lost *or* a time when you won a game.
565. "If you think I'm spending all day standing round in the cold while you play your silly game, you've another think coming . . ." Write a story including these words.
566. Choose a sport you've never tried. *Either* say why you think you might like to try it *or* why you don't want to.
567. "All sport should be professional." Do you agree?
568. What could be done to stop football hooliganism?
569. "Every summer, the country goes mad when two people hit a ball across a net for three hours on a sunny afternoon!" What's your view of tennis?
570. Do you think sport/games lessons at school should be compulsory? Why?
571. Write a story including one of the following: a rugby match, a sports centre, a lost ball, a cheat.
572. Write a story involving an important match, a broken leg and a last-minute rescue.
573. Write a story including a board game.
574. "I swung my arm back, threw the bowl . . . and forgot to let go. Elegantly, I slid the whole length of the alley!"
575. Write a description or a story involving a sporting occasion and lots of water.
576. Pretend you are a referee. Write about the worst match of your life.
577. Which sport do you enjoy playing most at school and which do you enjoy least? Why?

Towns and Cities

578. New Town	579. Lost in a Crowd	580. City Lights
581. The Underground	582. My Kind of Town	583. Hooligans!
584. City Limits	585. Future City	586. Pavement

587. Write about what's wrong with a town you know and suggest what could be done to help.
588. Describe your neighbourhood, trying to re-create the atmosphere.
589. Which is your favourite town? Why?
590. Write about one of the following, saying whether you think it is a good idea; traffic wardens, shopping centres, subways.
591. Write a description or a story in which a skyscraper plays an important part.
592. Pretend you are one of the following and describe some of the things you see and experience: a street trader, a kiosk assistant, a sales assistant in a take-away snack bar.
593. You are looking at a town you know from a good vantage point. Describe what you see.
594. Choose three of the following adjectives and use them to write a description of any aspect of life in a town: frantic, bustling, friendly, threatening, deserted, dusty, noisy, eerie, comforting.
595. Write a story involving a building, a bulldozer and a brick.
596. You are Minister for the Environment. Suggest three laws you would pass and say why you would choose them.
597. "I'll go mad if I stay in this town much longer!" Write a story including these words.
598. "He pulled into the town square, got out of the car and looked around. Everyone ignored his gaze . . ."
599. You can take a day trip to any city in the world. Which would you choose, what would you do there and why?
600. You wake up tomorrow to find your whole town deserted. Carry on the story from there.
601. You are walking through a town very early in the morning. Describe what you see and how you feel.
602. Describe an event, such as an annual procession or fair, where a whole town celebrates.
603. "The city was doomed. Nothing could save it now."

604. Rush Hour
605. Homeward Bound
606. The Passenger
607. Convoy
608. The Ferry
609. "Taxi!"
610. Hitch-hiking
611. Puncture
612. Hijack
613. My best journey ever
614. On the Buses
615. The Pedestrians strike back!
616. Railway station at dawn
617. You can spend a month's holiday wherever you want, money no object. Describe your holiday.
618. You've just spent a holiday visiting your pen-friend. Describe your experiences.
619. "Trains and boats and planes." Which do you prefer and why?
620. "As the train drew out of the station, I suddenly panicked." Carry on with this story.
621. Imagine you're a taxi driver or a bus conductor. Write about your work and the people you meet.
622. Draw a map showing your journey to school, then write about it.
623. Write about a day when something unusual happened during your journey to school – this could be real or make-believe.
624. Write a story which includes the words, "Do you think I travelled halfway round the world just to . . . ?"
625. Write a story ending with the words, "It's the last time I go on holiday with you!"
626. Write a story including two of the following: a lost passport, a delayed journey, a crash, a forgotten ticket, travel sickness.
627. All the petrol in the world has disappeared because of a vicious petrol virus that has escaped from a secret test laboratory. Write about what happens.
628. Write about a journey that you made in a mini-bus or coach.
629. Describe a journey that involved water.
630. You are going on a round-the-world trip. Plan your route, then describe where you would go and how you would travel from place to place.
631. Imagine you are the first person to leave the Solar System. Describe your experiences.
632. You are travelling from your home to London either two hundred years in the past or two hundred years in the future. Describe your journey.

Weather

633. Rain
634. Snowstorm
635. Misty
636. A Sunny Day
637. Fog in the City
638. The Thunderstorm
639. Heat Wave
640. Tidal Wave
641. Spring
642. Summer
643. Autumn
644. Winter
645. Drought!
646. Sunset
647. Hurricane

648. Wet pavements, umbrellas, the sound of falling rain. What are your memories of a rainy day?

649. "If only I'd brought my umbrella!" Write a story beginning with these words.

650. All of a sudden, the heavens opened . . . what happened next?

651. Write a story in which snow plays an important part.

652. White, silver, glistening, drifting, deep, soft, silent. . . Write a description of a snowy scene using as many good adjectives as you can.

653. If tomorrow was a free, sunny day, where would you spend the day and how?

654. Overnight, the climate of Britain changes completely. Imagine what the new climate is like, then describe how it would affect Britain.

655. By the year 4000, we control the weather. *Either* make suggestions as to how the weather could be better organised, *or* describe a typical day in your life in the year 4000.

656. "The fog slithered around everything, swiftly and silently, so that soon, all that could be seen was a thick, yellow blanket." Carry on from there, either a description or a story.

657. Write a story including a thick fog and any two of the following: a mad professor, a burglar, two old ladies, a lost child, a motorbike with a flat tyre.

658. Write a story beginning with the words, "There was a flash of lightning, a peal of thunder and . . ."

659. "The small boy came rushing towards us shrieking. Behind him, on the horizon, we could see a huge dark cloud." What happens next?

660. Have you ever woken up at dawn? Describe what you saw and how you felt.

661. Write about a place you know, describing how the seasons change it.

662. Which kind of weather do you like best? Why?

663. First Job   664. My Ideal Job   665. The Workers
666. Unemployment   667. The Interview   668. Nine to Five
669. The Factory   670. Office Life   671. First Day at Work
672. You are a worker in the year 2500. Describe your day's work as *either* a nurse *or* a firefighter.
673. You read this advertisement in the newspaper. "WANTED – bright young person willing to take risks, for unusual job involving travel and action." What happens next?
674. Describe a job interview where everything goes wrong.
675. Write a story beginning with the words, "Work, work, work –that's all I ever do!"
676. Choose three of these and include them in a story: a cross boss, a leaving present, a pay rise, an office party, a promotion, a sulky office junior, a canteen meal.
677. Are careers opportunities equal for boys and girls?
678. Write a story about someone who didn't have to work.
679. Should men stay at home and women go out to work?
680. "I have to work for the next forty years of my life, but women can stay at home. It isn't fair!" Do you agree?
681. Why do we have to work? Write your ideas on the subject.
682. The day I got the sack.
683. The day I nearly lost my job.
684. What would you do with your life if you didn't have to work?
685. Describe a typical day's work at school.
686. Which job would you most hate to do and why?
687. Write a story about two people sharing the same job and the funny things that happen.
688. Pretend you are a careers officer. Describe a typical day at work.
689. Do you think 55 would be a good age to retire? Why or why not?
690. "I'm really glad I retired." Write a story including these words.
691. In the middle of your working day, the boss asks you to go to her office. Carry on the story from there.
692. A friend tells you he or she is having problems at work. Write giving him or her your advice.
693. What was your first ambition? What do you think of that job now?

694. Far Away
695. The Gas Man Cometh
696. White Elephant
697. Knuckle Sandwich
698. A Sporting Chance
699. Black is Black
700. Room at the Top
701. After the Rain Stopped
702. Too Many Cooks
703. A Rolling Stone
704. The Acid Test
705. Make or Break
706. Pot Luck
707. Fool's Paradise
708. Life or Death
709. On the War-Path
710. Trial and Error
711. A Chip off the Old Block
712. In the Dark
713. Caught Red-Handed
714. Courage of Convictions
715. Out of Sight, Out of Mind
716. Making Both Ends Meet
717. Castles in the Air
718. On the Side-Lines
719. Rogues' Gallery
720. Never Say Die
721. The Black Sheep
722. A Pat on the Back
723. The Gift Horse
724. Golden Opportunity
725. Small Talk
726. Humble Pie
727. Jolly Roger
728. Spur of the Moment

729. The Old Hand
730. Red Letter Day
731. Written Off
732. A Put-Up Job
733. All Present and Correct
734. Rock Bottom
735. Out of the Frying Pan
736. Turning In
737. Fair and Square
738. I Wonder
739. An Ill Wind
740. Bear with a Sore Head
741. Just Common Sense
742. Man of the World
743. Island in the Sun
744. A Tall Story
745. The Last Straw
746. Plain Sailing
747. Out to Lunch
748. The Right Track
749. Behind the Times
750. Turning a Blind Eye
751. Facing the Music
752. Turn for the Worse
753. Out in the Cold
754. A Dog's Life
755. The Also-Ran
756. Spilt Milk
757. More than I Bargained for
758. Last Resort
759. Heads I Win
760. The Impossible Dream
761. Better Late than Never
762. Thick and Thin
763. The Last Word

764. Perhaps we could . . .
765. It's beyond me how . . .
766. The only thing I ever . . .
767. I hope that . . .
768. I wonder if . . .
769. I can't get over . . .
770. She's talking about . . .
771. I remember when . . .
772. Look at this . . .
773. It's a secret, but . . .
774. It's a bit like . . .
775. It's strange that . . .
776. There it is . . .
777. Only you could . . .
778. I whispered . . .
779. Are you . . .
780. There are four . . .
781. While I was . . .
782. He hissed . . .
783. I hate . . .
784. Welcome to . . .
785. They screamed . . .
786. She said coldly . . .
787. Open the door or . . .
788. Please pass the . . .
789. Trust him to . . .
790. Where's the . . .
791. This is the end . . .
792. Listen to . . .
793. Hurry up or . . .
794. He sobbed . . .
795. We've got a surprise . . .
796. Why are you . . .
797. Let's stay, in case . . .
798. It's funny that . . .
799. Face facts or . . .
800. Then she said . . .
801. I've just found . . .
802. I voted for . . .
803. If only . . .
804. She stated firmly that . . .
805. It's impossible to . . .
806. He shouted . . .
807. With luck, I'll . . .
808. Just look out . . .
809. I disagree . . .
810. That's mine, and . . .
811. Maybe if . . .
812. Try . . .
813. Let me go . . .
814. They explained . . .
815. Tell me why . . .
816. My problem is that . . .
817. Suppose that . . .
818. I'll see you at . . .
819. He did it because . . .
820. It looks as though . . .
821. The trouble is . . .
822. Mind the . . .
823. It's amazing how . . .
824. Don't break the . . .
825. Just in case . . .
826. There's a message saying . . .
827. Have you been . . .
828. I keep meeting . . .
829. I can't promise to . . .
830. I protest against
831. Where on earth . . .
832. I want to say . . .
833. Yesterday we . . .

834. Accident
835. Ace
836. Afternoon
837. Applause
838. Arrival
839. Bat
840. Bomb
841. Brake
842. Brush-Off
843. Campaign
844. Capsize
845. Carelessness
846. Car Salesman
847. Catastrophe
848. Celebrity
849. Censorship
850. Challenge
851. Chase
852. Choice
853. Christmas
854. Commando
855. Confusion
856. Copycat
857. Culprit
858. Curtains
859. Deadlock
860. Defeat
861. Dentist
862. Descent
863. Disappeared
864. Discovery
865. Doctor
866. Duel
867. Dynamite
868. Eccentric

869. Enemy
870. Energy
871. Exhibition
872. Expedition
873. Explosion
874. Fair
875. Fall
876. Fence
877. Festival
878. Fight
879. Final
880. Fined
881. Fire
882. Fly
883. Fool
884. Foreigner
885. Forest
886. Foundation
887. Freedom
888. Gift
889. Gipsy
890. Glamour
891. Heartbreak
892. Heat
893. Hello
894. Hero
895. Highway
896. Hold-Up
897. Holiday
898. Hospital
899. Hotel
900. Ice
901. Illuminations
902. Impostor
903. Invitation

904. Jam
905. Jealousy
906. Journey
907. Jungle
908. Key
909. Late
910. Lesson
911. Library
912. Lie
913. Light
914. Loneliness
915. Magic
916. Map
917. Master
918. Memories
919. Mine
920. Mole
921. Money
922. Mountain
923. Moving
924. Newcomer
925. Nurse
926. Ordeal
927. Overboard
928. Padlock
929. Painting
930. Parade
931. Parasite
932. Parcel
933. Pardon
934. Passer-by
935. Path
936. Phantom
937. Photograph
938. Play

939. Plotters
940. Poltergeist
941. Pop
942. Post
943. Poster
944. Powerhouse
945. Prediction
946. Press
947. Prize
948. Problem
949. Protest
950. Question
951. Rally
952. Rebel
953. Reception
954. Rejection
955. Rendezvous
956. Replay
957. Rescue
958. Reunion
959. Revision
960. Rumour
961. Runaway
962. Saved
963. Search
964. Secretary
965. Shambles
966. Silence
967. Snap
968. Snob
969. Solo
970. Souvenir
971. Speech
972. Strike
973. Subway

In a Word

Printed and bound in Great Britain by
William Clowes (Beccles) Limited, Beccles and London